ENQUIRING MINDS... want to KNOW

A catalogue record for this book is available from the British Library.

First Edition 2017. Written by Patrick Potter

First published in Great Britain in 2017 by Carpet Bombing Culture.

An imprint of Pro-actif Communications.

Email: books@carpetbombingculture.co.uk

ISBN: 978-1-908211-52-1

CARPET
BOMBING
CULTURE

www.carpetbombingculture.co.uk

ASK ME
ASK ME
ASK ME

Random Questions for
Awesome Conversations

HOW TO USE THIS BOOK?

No, we're asking you.
We're not entirely sure.

JOKES

Or is it?

Well you have to know the rules before you can break them. So we made these rules up for you to break so you can feel like a maverick outsider. That's how much we care about you.

This book is tiny for a reason.
Keep it in your bag.
Open it at random and randomly fire questions at random people.

Pass the book around.
Take turns at asking.
Use it when hanging out in real space.
Use it when hanging out in cyberspace.

Use it to make new friends.
Use it to learn more about old friends or family. Use it to make video interviews for your socials. Use it creatively.
Use it whenever you're bored.

STAY PLAYFUL

Above all - talk to each other. It's fun.

YOU AND YOUR FRIENDS ARE JUST AS INTERESTING AS ANYONE WHO HAS EVER LIVED.

Let the Question Games Begin!

PLAYAAAA
AAAAAAA

AAAAAAA

!!!!!!!!!!!

There are four sections within this book and we encourage you to play each one as follows . . .

FUN FACTS

Decisions, decisions, decisions. Do your prefer cats or dogs? These sections are packed with questions designed to pry out hard factual data from all your interviewees. Ask one person or throw them out to the group like some random crazy questions geek.

CHAT SHOW

Slow it down a little. Let's really get under your guest's skin. Turn the world into your very own chat show couch. Ideal for one-to-one use either with a live audience or without. Great for people who ain't shy and like talking about themselves. You are allowed to think before you answer...

RAPID FIRE / RANDOM QUESTIONS

Choose your victim. (You may choose yourself).
Take aim and fire. Rapid and random questions to
be answered QUICKLY without THINKING TOO
MUCH. Oops! Did I say that out loud?

SHOW STOPPERS

For those who are sick of small talk and want to
take the conversation deeper. Drop one of these
babies on the table at the smoothie bar and watch
the conversation blow up.

Use with caution. May make people think.

MAY THE QUESTIONS BE WITH YOU...

You have learned everything
we can teach you. You must go now.

The book is yours.

Do as you will with it.

To each question master their own style.

WHAT IS THE SECRET
OF BEING
FASCINATING?
BE
FASCINATED!

FUN FACTS

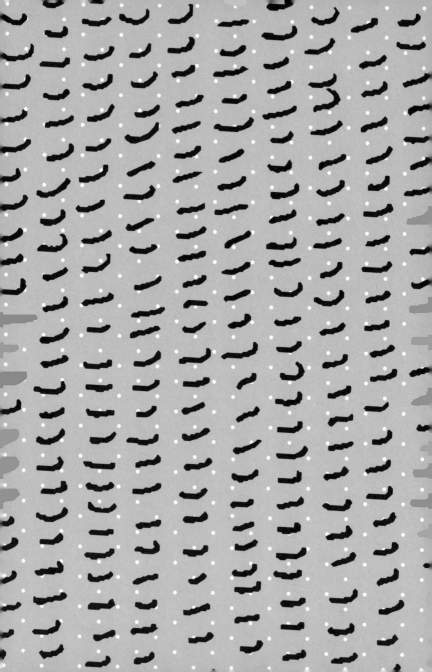

Decisions, decisions, decisions.

Do your prefer cats or dogs?

These sections are packed with questions
designed to pry out hard factual data
from all your interviewees.

Ask one person or throw them out to the group
like some random crazy questions geek.

FUN FACTS ABOUT YOU

A billion years ago, before the internets came out of the mountain, young people would sit around reading magazines together and asking each other questions. It was a dark and difficult time when people had to listen to each other because there was nothing, literally nothing else to do. It's difficult to imagine now how hard life was for those people. They are probably all dead now.

Nowadays of course nobody can read and everybody thinks in a series of flickering animated gifs, cheesy quotes and Pinterest boards. The only thing people ever say to each other is 'have you got an iPhone charger?'

Luckily for you, as you are more intelligent and good looking than almost everybody else in the world, you have sourced this book into your personal stash of amazing life tools.

Most people have never heard of a book. Not you.

With this treasure trove of fun factual questions sourced directly from the type of thing that would definitely have gone into early 1990's magazine questionnaires you can now relive the early 1990's.

Lock away all your phones. Get all your friends together in your room. Stare at the ceiling until you are so bored you literally start crying.

Now open up the fun facts sections in this book.

Spend a ridiculously long time asking all your friends and writing down their answers with a pencil in the back of an old school text book. I mean really milk it.

See if you can get Kylie Minogue's first album on cassette and you'll basically be there.

Mom calls you downstairs to answer the phone...

...and you actually have to go downstairs to answer the phone.

YAAAAAA
AAAAAAAA
AAAAAAS

The player who can answer yes to the most questions is elected the president of the universe.

1. Do you use all your mobile data on pointless YouTube videos?

2. Do you never want to grow up?

3. Do you try to save money then accidentally order random nonsense off the internet late at night?

4. Do you swear you are going to stay in and do loads of work then spend the whole evening on Instagram / SnapChat / Musical.ly / etc.?

5. Do you spend hours hanging out in the park with your friends not actually talking to each other but just showing each other things on your phones?

6. Do you have sudden random impulses that lead to regrettable yet hilarious incidents which your 'friends' helpfully livestream?

7. Have you ever secretly wished you were born long before the internet existed?

8. Do you regret having uploaded anything to the internet when you were younger that now seems unintentionally hilarious to all your friends?

continued...

9. Have you ever deleted all your social media accounts only to open new ones less than a week later?

10. Have you ever been on late night missions to unfriend swathes of your contacts based on a weird arbitrary criteria that seemed to be important at the time?

11. Do you take your phone to bed?

12. Do you carry a portable power bank?

13. Have you ever made or attempted to make your own meme?

14. Have you ever watched a video of somebody else playing a computer game?

15. Have you ever made a hair / make-up tutorial?

16. Have you ever asked anyone 'How many followers do you have?'

17. Do you say things that come from the internet, such as 'on fleek'?

18. Do you ever dream of the internet?

SAVE AND DESTROY 1

Save one and the other is erased from existence.
Pizza or Chips? Save Pizza! Chips are gone.
Like, forever. It's your fault.

Money *or* Fame

Waffles *or* Pancakes

Sunrise *or* Sunset

Head *or* Heart

Call *or* Text

Pizza *or* Pasta

Snapchat *or* Pinterest

The Book *or* The Movie

Board Games *or* Video Games

Cats *or* Dogs

Super Hero *or* Super Villain

Pepsi *or* Coke

Sitcom *or* Documentary?

Books *or* TV?

Tea *or* Coffee?

Go Invisible *or* Be Able to Fly?

Sporty *or* Arty?

WOULD YOU RATHER?

Your fairy godmother appears and offers you a choice between two gifts...

1. Would you rather be a great singer *or* a great dancer?

2. Would you rather be weird looking and confident *or* normal looking and shy?

3. Would you rather be really attractive *or* really funny?

4. Would you rather be very strong *or* very smart?

5. Would you rather be 3 inches taller *or* 3 inches shorter?

6. Would you rather have great teeth *or* great hair?

7. Would you rather have an small apartment in a cool city *or* a huge house in the middle of nowhere?

8. Would you rather be super-intelligent *or* better looking?

GAP DAT?

Fill in the BLANKS with those 'word' things that people seem to like.

1. When I *BLANK* I really really *BLANK*.

2. I've always wanted to be *BLANK*.

3. I'll never forget that *BLANK*.

4. I'm so freaking bored of *BLANK* right now.

5. And then he said *BLANK* and then she said *BLANK*.

6. I saw *BLANK* the other day and I thought of you.

7. I'm so desperate to buy a new *BLANK*.

8. I think I'm falling in love with *BLANK*.

9. I think my friend *BLANK* is in love with *BLANK*.

10. I cannot wait to go to *BLANK*.

11. I'm kinda hoping that *BLANK* will *BLANK*.

HERE ARE SOME MORE THINGS AND YOU MUST CHOOSE THE BEST ONE

Starter, Main Course *or* Dessert

MP3, CD, Vinyl *or* Cassette Tape

Samsung, Sony *or* Apple (phones)

Beach, City Break, Adventure, Skiing *or* Cruise

Be happy but poor *or* Rich and miserable

Cat, Dog, Rabbit, Goldfish *or* Canary

Late Nights *or* Early Mornings

Tokyo, NY, London, Rome, Barcelona, LA *or* Paris

Spring, Summer, Autumn *or* Winter

IF YOU HAD TO CHOOSE ONE

Or you would be exiled to the moon forever.
Which would you choose?

Real Camera or Phone Camera?

Playstation or Xbox?

Nike or Adidas?

Series or Movies?

Instagram or Snapchat?

Live Music or Live Sport?

Dress up or Dress down?

Comic Convention or Gaming Convention?

Making Stuff or Buying Stuff?

Puppies or Kittens?

Creativity or Knowledge?

Save or Spend?

Early Bird or Night Owl?

Brothers or Sisters?

Black or Pink?

DREAMING
OF YOU...

Find out exactly who should be your future life partner. No money back guarantee.

Jocks or Geeks?

Cute or Beautiful?

Thoughtful or Funny?

Dark or Fair?

Popular or Deep?

Arty or Sciencey?

Comforting or Exciting?

Stable or Adventurous?

Street or Preppy?

Cheeky or Mysterious?

Realist or Dreamer?

Taller than you or Shorter?

Pay the bill or Go halves?

Skinny or Chunky?

Smart or Scruffy?

Eyes or Smile?

THE BRIDE
OF FRANKENSTEIN

*If you could construct your own Prince Charming /
Disney Princess, where would you source the parts?*

The eyes of:

The hair of:

The smile of:

The body of:

The skin of:

The style of:

The dance moves of:

The laugh of:

The sense of humour of:

The talents of:

The brains of:

The charm of:

BANTS.

SIC. BANTER – BRITISH COLLOQUIAL,
BANTEROUS EXCHANGE, JAPES, JOKES,
VERBAL TOMFOOLERY, LARKS,
THE TRADING OF WITTICISMS
AND NONSENSE IN THE PURSUIT
OF LOLS.
ALSO SEE CRAIC.

BACKWARDS
THIS GAME IS

Here are the answers.
You invent the questions.
For the lols.

I'm doing great thanks for asking.

Burberry.

Justin Bieber.

About thirty thousand.

You can't deny the value of their work.

I refuse to answer that.

Only on a Thursday night.

Roughly seventy-five percent.

Pull yourself together.

Oh yes, that is definitely me.

My family.

HERE ARE SOME MORE THINGS AND YOU MUST CHOOSE THE BEST ONE

Internet, TV, Gaming, Music *or* Sport

Boiled, Scrambled, Sunny Side Up *or* Over Easy

One wish now *or* Three wishes in 10 years time

Star Wars I, II, III, IV, V, VI *or* VII

Sunrise *or* Sunset

Dance, Indie, Hip Hop, Pop *or* Rock

Good News First *or* Bad News First

Museum, Gallery, Gig *or* Theme Park

The Beginning *or* The End

50's, 60's, 70's, 80's, 90's *or* 00's

WHO SHOULD YOU RIDE OFF INTO THE SUNSET WITH?

The only way you can possibly know is to immediately rate the importance of the following features out of ten. Then throw an apple skin over your left shoulder and look in the mirror at midnight.

Ability to talk about emotions: /10

Ability to communicate with subtle glances: /10

Ability to make you laugh until you snort in a disturbing manner: /10

Ability to make you feel really important: /10

Ability to make you feel that life is full of possibilities: /10

Ability to shut up and make supportive noises when required: /10

Ability to dance: /10

Ability to sing: /10

Ability to take excellent photographs: /10

Ability to make money: /10

Ability to share your interests: /10

Ability to work hard: /10

Ability to play hard: /10

Ability to chill hard: /10

Knowledge of digital technology: /10

Knowledge of music: /10

Knowledge of sports: /10

Knowledge of art: /10

Knowledge of TV: /10

Knowledge of movies: /10

Knowledge of current events: /10

Knowledge of politics: /10

continued...

...continued

Loyalty: /10

Kindness: /10

Consideration: /10

Courage: /10

Toughness: /10

Independence: /10

Beliefs: /10

Values: /10

Ambition: /10

Stability: /10

Spontaneity: /10

Imagination: /10

Reason: /10

Passion: /10

Sense of fun: /10

Now you know what you're looking for
. . . it should be easy!

CURIOSITY thrilled THE CATS

WOULD YOU RATHER?

Your fairy godmother appears again...

1. Would you rather be a one hit wonder *or* an undiscovered genius?

2. Would you rather make art *or* technology?

3. Would you rather have a stable job *or* be your own boss?

4. Would you rather be lucky in love *or* lucky in business?

5. Would you rather be famous *or* rich?

6. Would you rather be loved *or* powerful?

7. Would you rather be in the spotlight *or* working behind the scenes?

8. Would you rather be an awesome cook *or* eat out every night?

9. Would you rather be answering this question *or* asking it?

GAP DAT?

Fill in the BLANKS with those 'word' things that people seem to like.

1. So if *BLANK BLANKS* then do you think *BLANK* will *BLANK*?

2. Wait guys, I've got it! Our new band name is *BLANK BLANK*.

3. And our first album is gonna be *BLANK BLANK BLANK*.

4. I think my *BLANK* is my best feature.

5. And then the whole place just went *BLANK*.

6. My mind has gone *BLANK*.

7. Is it just me, or does *BLANK* seem like a really weird word now?

BLANK BLANK BLANK

Mic drop.

I'm out.

BRANDTASTIC 1

*Which is your favourite brand
for each of these must have items and services?*

Sneaks / Creps / Trainers / Tennis Shoes?

Portable Cellular Smart Telephone?

High Street Retailer?

High Street Restaurant?

Jacket / Coat?

Jeans?

Tracksuit?

Hoody?

Hat / Cap?

Leisurewear?

Eveningwear?

YOU CANNOT SAY
YES OR NO

*Try to answer all the questions
without saying yes or no.*

Hi, how are you?

Are you OK?

Are you ready to play?

Have we started yet?

What does n-o spell?

Does n-o spell yes?

Oh so that's y-e-s?

Y-e-s or n-o?

You're good at this right?

You feel like a winner?

What's your name?

Who are you?

AND NOW
YOU MUST LIE

Ask every question in rapid fire.
Answer every question with a bare faced lie.

Are you happy to be here?

What is your name?

Where were you born?

Where did you grow up?

Who is your best friend?

What is really important to you?

What makes you laugh?

Do you love unicorns?

How many unicorns do you own?

Do you have unicorn bedsheets?

And unicorn curtains?

And unicorn wallpaper?

And unicorn pyjamas?

Do you believe that unicorns are real?

Do you love them?

What about mermaids?

Do you have any tattoos?

Are they of mermaids?

What do you think of Nicki Minaj?

Who is your favourite recording artist?

Who is your favourite YouTuber?

Why do you love their work so much?

What do you really think of me?

Who do you have a crush on right now?

Do you want me to put that on Facebook?

Are you lying to me?

YOU HAVE TO SAY YES

*You must swear by the moon
to answer yes to every single question.*

Hi, how are you?

What's your name?

That's a lovely name.

Are you a special person?

That's nice.

Am I like a personal hero to you?

Do you often think about me?

Do you wonder how awesome it would be to be
me for a little while?

OK you can be me for a while.

How does it feel?

I thought so.

BACKWARDS
THIS GAME IS

Here are the answers.
You invent the questions.
For the lols.

I want to concentrate on my work right now.

South Korea.

Jeggings.

Stay classy.

Ben and Jerry's Cookie Dough Flavour.

Her makeup looks terrible.

If you have to ask you'll never know.

I'll give you his number.

For the lulz.

42.

The back end of a bus.

Your mom.

BRANDTASTIC 2

*Which is your favourite brand
for each of these must have items and services?*

Bag / Purse?

Sunglasses?

Tablet / Laptop?

Games Console?

Make Up?

Jewellery?

Scent / Perfume?

Hair Products?

Social Media?

Car / Motorbike / Truck?

Bicycle / Scooter / Skateboard?

YOU CANNOT SAY
YES OR NO

Try to answer all the questions
without saying yes or no.

What time is it?

Is it OK say know?

No, not no I said know.

So how do I know if you say know or no?

I don't no.

Do you no?

OK you win, yes?

So it's over now, right?

We can stop this now, yes?

Is it better to know or not know?

If the game is over...

It's OK I hate me too.

YOU HAVE TO SAY YES

*You must swear by the moon
to answer yes to every single question.*

You are out of control.

Do you want to sing for us?

OK go ahead.

Can I have that?

Do you stalk me on the internet?

Can we livestream this interview on Youtube?

So, are we having a party at your house tonight?

Are you going to pick me up?

Would you like this to stop now?

What is the most intelligent thing you can say
right now?

You realise you're shaming your family right now?

Go to bed and think about what you have done.

SAVE AND DESTROY 2

You know the drill.
Save one and the other is erased from existence.

Call or Text?

Romantic or Realistic?

Rock or Hip Hop?

Digital or Analogue?

Retro or Contemporary?

America or Europe?

Asia or Africa?

Fairies or Unicorns?

Apple or Android?

Thrift Store or Flagship Store?

Maths or English?

Beach Holiday or City Break?

Action or Relaxation?

Butter or Spread?

Meat or Vegetables?

Kanye or Beyonce?

Swimming or Cake?

Colouring Books or Sketch Books?

It's now time to slow it down a little.

Let's really get under your guest's skin.

Turn the world into your very own
chat show couch.

Ideal for one-to-one use
either with a live audience or without.

Great for people who ain't shy and
like talking about themselves.

You are allowed to think before you answer...

YOUR OWN PERSONAL CHAT SHOW

It's really late. You should have switched off your screen hours ago. The whole internet is stale copypasta. If you see one more 'try not to laugh video' you'll claw out your own eyes. If anybody else whines about you breaking their streak you're going to kill the internet with a hammer. Wait! It doesn't have to be this way!

What if you used the most powerful communication tools ever created to...communicate!

Try this. It'll change your digital life.

Pick someone you ACTUALLY CARE ABOUT.

Send them a message a little like this one...

Hey! I cannot tell you how excited I am to have you on my show! This is the interview I have waited my whole career for!

I'm going to interview you live on (Insert Social Media Channel) so please make yourself comfortable on my imaginary couch.
How the heck are you doing?

Now let's get into it...

Pick a Chat Show section from this book.
Feed your questions one by one to your guest.
Ask follow up questions. Think like Oprah.

This is ordinary magic. People blossom when you pay them attention.

If the book is training wheels you can take them off as soon as you are ready to ride alone.

Flood the internet with interesting conversations.
Make life better online for everyone.

Some Ideas for creating your own Online Interviews

1. Send questions on Snapchat.

2. Film questions to post to FB.

3. Encourage people to film responses.

4. Do it live and direct on YouTube Live / Periscope / FB / (*insert your own live streaming service here*).

5. Send questions as audio files on WhatsApp.

6. Start your own podcast.

7. Start your own Tumblr.

INTERROGATION IS THE HIGHEST FORM of FLATTERY.

GET ON MY DANG COUCH!

HEY YOU! GET ON MY DANG COUCH!

I am your host for this evening and you are my fabulous guest. I cannot tell you how *EXCITED I AM* to have you here.

You have to ask AT LEAST TWO penetrating yet flattering follow-up questions.
If you can't think of one - JUST REPEAT THE LAST FEW WORDS that your interviewee said in a questioning tone. It always works.

If you can get your interviewee to talk for two full minutes you win

ALL THE PRIZES.

TURN UP...

*Questions about #party. And the meaning of life.
Which is #party.*

1. Tell us about the greatest party
   you ever hosted

2. The best party you ever went to

3. The worst party you ever went to

4. What is the ultimate party playlist?

5. Give us your top tips for party survival

6. If you had a 100,000 to spend on one party...?

7. What is the most #party thing about you?

8. Do your parents party?

9. Where is the line between 'life of the party'
   and 'party casualty'

10. What song should be playing when you arrive
    at the party?

...AND
TURN OUT

11. Why is the kitchen the best place to be?

12. How do you get everybody to dance?

13. Which 3 celebs would you have at your party?

14. Who are your party wingmen?

15. Who should be manning the decks at your party.

16. Help with the clean up or run away?

17. What do you put in the party bags?

18. What is the next party you are likely to attend?

19. What song would you drop to send the party people crazy?

20. You're at a party in heaven. Describe it.

I CANNOT EVEN

I just cannot. Not even. I can't with you. I am so cannot with this. All of this. SO many nopes.

Anger. Keep it in or let it out?

Five things in your life that should not be.

Most irritating person you know.

Annoying things people do on social media.

Last time you lost your temper.

Last time you #ragequit a game.

Show us your angry but trying to be polite face.

Do you storm off dramatically?

Rate your drama.

One thing that drives you nuts.

Do you secretly enjoy drama?

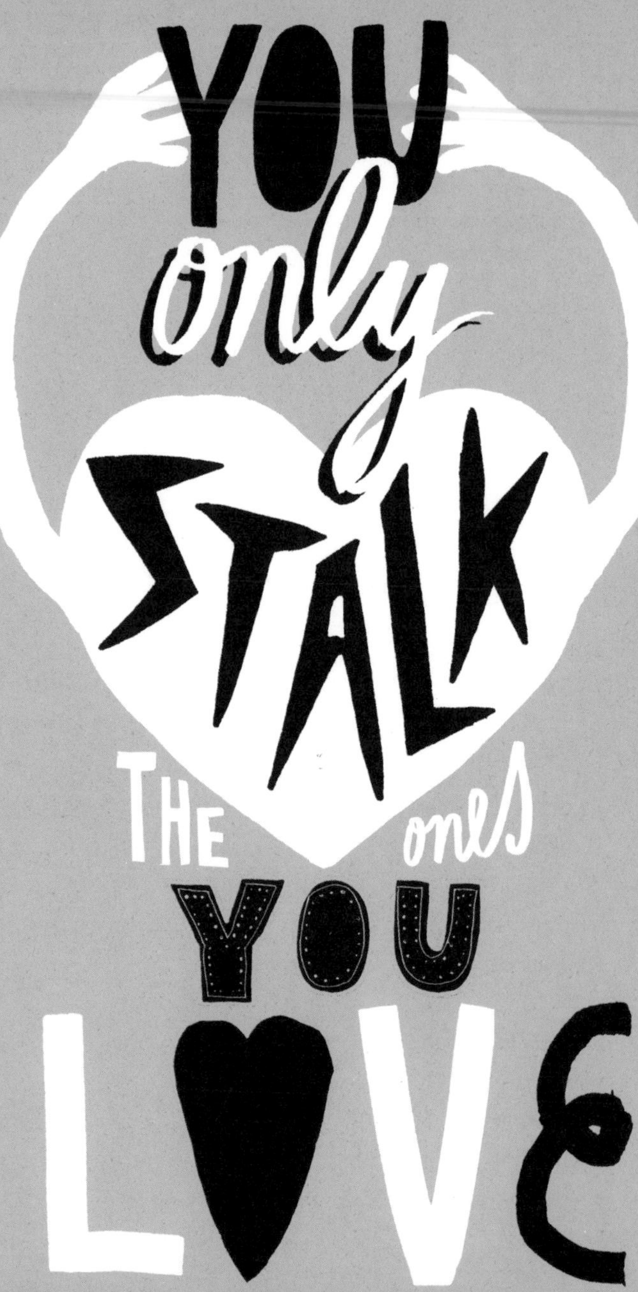
YOU only STALK THE ones YOU LOVE

ARE
THE RUMOURS
TRUE?

*You've been seen in photographs
with megastar X.*

*You've photoshopped yourself
into red carpet receptions together.*

Is it true that you're in an imaginary relationship?

1. In your imaginary life who is your celebrity life partner and why?

2. Which celebs would you matchmake your best friends with?

3. Which famous person would you secretly love to be?

4. Which celebrity relationship makes you sigh and daydream?

5. Have you ever been upset by a celebrity break-up?

6. Who is your celebrity style guru?

7. If you could be adopted by a celebrity, who would it be?

8. Which five famous people do you invite to your next birthday party and why?

9. When you get famous, who will you move in next door to? Who is your ideal celebrity next door neighbour?

10. Where do you go on imaginary holiday / vacation with your celeb crush?

11. What inadvisable movie vanity project do you produce with your celeb crush?

12. What is your song? (In your imaginary celeb relationship)

13. What is the % chance of any of this actually happening?

I CANNOT EVEN

I just cannot. Not even. I can't with you. I am so cannot with this. All of this. SO many nopes.

Complain out loud or simmer in silent rage?

Negotiate or go on the warpath?

Do you tolerate fools?

Are you good at calming yourself?

How do you self-soothe?

Are these questions annoying you?

Shall I stop now?

How about now?

How about now?

Your eyes have gone scary. I'll just get my coat.

#runsaway

Every time you DODGE...

A question a PUPPY gets SICK!

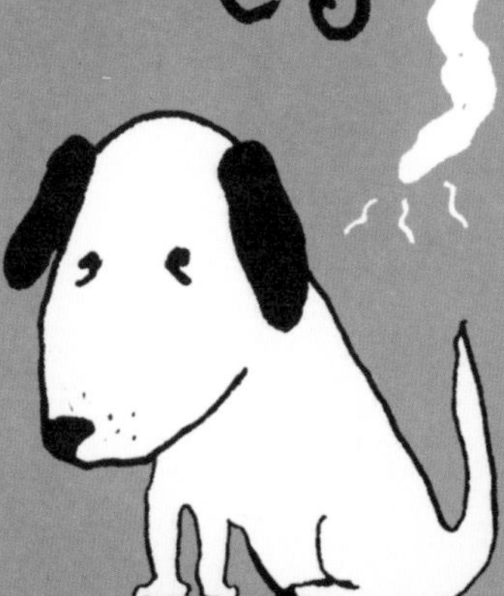

LIGHTS!
CAMERA!
ACTION!

Your life as a movie!

Hollywood has come knocking at your door and it wants to make a movie of your life.

There's a massive budget and its going to be epic. You are brought in as executive casting director, so:

What is the movie title?

Which film star plays the part of you?

What song plays in the opening titles?

Which film star plays your best friend?

Who directs the movie?

What certificate is it?

What song is the main theme song?

Who is the villain of the movie?

Which film star plays the villain?

Who is the hero of the movie?

Which film star plays the hero?

What song plays in the closing credits?

I CANNOT EVEN

I just cannot. Not even. I can't with you. I am so cannot with this. All of this. SO many nopes. Who and what can you just <u>not</u> deal with right now?

Which relative?

Which current trend?

Which meme?

Which commercial / advert?

Which feature of modern life?

Which aspect of school?

Which ongoing argument?

Which frenemy?

Which song?

Which thing you own?

Which food?

Which unrealistic parental expectation?

Which celebrity?

Which obsession?

Which bad habit?

Which patronising adult attitude to young people?

Which dumb question you keep getting asked?

#hashtag OMG!

—THE—

META-HASHTAG

THE MEME WITHIN THE MEME

TEKSMEBAK

Yeah? You receive the following teks.
What do you teksbak?

On a scale of one to America how free are you tonight?

Wassup babygurl!?

You make me wanna knit us matching sweaters.

I can't believe they let me text during the exam!

Switch your phone off sweety you have school in the morning.

So we hittin the burger bar or what?

I'm at the store. What goldfish do you want?

This goat is eating your chair. Can I shoot it now?

I'm looking forward to yesterday!

Thanks for signing up to CAT FACTS. You will now receive fun daily facts about CATS!

Everything has gone according to plan. Be ready.

Surrounded by coyotes, your poncho will help.

Oye loca ?? Sabes donde he dejado mis calcetines rayadas??

It's done. She's gone.

ACTIVATE
PLAN NATHAN

Come over now. I think I found an entrance to Narnia.

I've changed my mind. Let's go.

Hey I think I found your phone down the back of my couch.

Can I practice my karate on you?

RAPID FIRE
AND
RANDOM
QUESTIONS

Choose your victim.

(You may choose yourself.)

Take aim and fire.

Twenty rapid and random questions
to be answered QUICKLY
without THINKING TOO MUCH.

Oops!

Did I say that out loud?

THINK FAST!
RAPID FIRE AND
RANDOM QUESTIONS

Choose your victim! These collections of random questions are designed to be asked and answered quickly. Do <u>not</u> pause. Do <u>not</u> think. Best used with a crowd of trusted amigos. Can you answer all the questions without spilling any beans?

Say the first thing that comes into your head.

As you race to keep up with the QUESTIONAGEDDON you will get a little dizzy and possibly even accidentally tell the truth.

Oh wait. Did I just say that out loud? You'll surprise you friends. Maybe you'll even surprise yourself.

Like a party game in your pocket - 'Think Fast' will liven up the banter in any situation. Take turns. Pass the book around. It's only fair if you answer the questions too. Keep it snappy. Have fun.

Warning. These questions can be revealing. Use carelessly. Contrary to popular belief - you can be too careful.

LIKE,
IS
that
EVEN A
THING

BIG

FAT

SMALL TALK

*Because sometimes it's nice to talk about
absolutely nothing that matters.*

What are you wearing right now?

Where did you get it?

How much is your whole outfit worth?

How many brands are you wearing?

Rate your look.

What are your colours?

Can you wear hats?

What is your favourite garment?

How long does it take you to get dressed?

What is the first thing that comes into your head
right now?

What is your party trick?

What is your best dance move?

Which is your least favourite cheese?

Celebrity crush?

Name one thing you suck at.

The last thing you made.

NOTHING IS TRIVIAL

*Because the universe is right there
in that grain of sand, baby.*

1. Who is the most famous person you have met?

2. Favourite kids TV show?

3. Who was your first best friend?

4. What's your favourite ice cream flavour?

5. Which book would you like to read again?

6. What is your current word of the moment?

7. Give me one word that describes the place where you live?

8. What was your favourite subject at school?

9. What is the weirdest thing you've ever eaten?

10. Who was your favourite teacher?

11. What is the best album of all time?

12. What is the best single of all time?

13. What is your current favourite show?

14. Who was your least favourite teacher?

15. Who is your favourite band of all time?

IF YOU WERE A ?
WHICH ?
WOULD YOU BE?

Which music video would you be?

Which book would you be?

What movie would you be?

Which famous person would you be?

Which designer label would you be?

Which band would you be?

Which album would you be?

Which song would you be?

Which TV series would you be?

Which superhero comic character are you?

Which Disney character are you?

MY

BIG

FAT

SCHOOL QUIZ

Tell us all about your edukayshon!

Name of school?

Uniform (or not)?

Best teacher?

Worst teacher?

Funniest teacher?

Favourite class?

Best work you ever did...

Worst fail...

Most embarrassing moment...

Best friends...

School crush...

School hero...

The popular kids?

The cool kids?

Describe your best ever school trip.

Were you in any school clubs?

Most intelligent thing you can remember
being taught...

Most useless thing you have been taught...

The stuff you just cannot remember...

What career would you love to have?

IMPORTANT QUESTIONS ABOUT CHEESE

1. Describe your life using only a movie title.

2. Which is your favourite cheese?

3. What is your party trick?

4. What do you find yourself doing a lot these days?

5. What is your current obsession?

6. Can you describe the way that you dance in one word?

7. Do you make things?

8. What is the first thing that comes into your head right now?

9. Can you make a prediction about something one year from now?

10. What do you do on Saturdays?

11. Where is your favourite place to hang out?

12. Are there any of the cheeses which you do not care for?

LIFE is better WHEN YOU ASK MORE Questions.

I GOTTA
GOTTA GOTTA
GOTTA
CRUSH ON
YOOOOOOOO

What are you really bad at?

Are there real monsters in the world?

What do you love the most about your town?

What's the most fun thing you do at home?

What is your most cherished possession?

What's your favourite children's TV programme
from when you were little?

Who was your best friend at primary school?

What can money not buy?

What is the one thing you could never
live without?

Something you do that you could never give up?

Is there a new hobby you would like to start
one day?

Who is your celebrity crush?

If you house was on fire, what item
would you grab?

IRRITATING ALIEN ICE CREAM

1. What's your favourite ice cream flavour?

2. Which book would you like to read again?

3. What is your current word of the moment?

4. Describe yourself in three words.

5. What irritates you?

6. Who is your team?

7. Give me one word that describes the place where you live?

8. What is the weirdest thing you've ever eaten?

9. What scares you the most?

10. What is your trigger?

11. Do you believe in aliens?

12. Who was your favourite teacher?

13. What is the best album of all time?

14. What is the best single of all time?

WORD UP!

The mind is a mysterious thing.
Let's see what's going on in yours.
Using word association, choose one word
for the following . . . and quickly!

Future

Crazy

School

Normal

Home

Overrated

Hero

Holiday

Bliss

Trend

Boring

Success

Dumb

Perfect

Like

KILLING IT IN THE GYM.

IT'S PART OF MY LIFE

1. Who is the most fashionable person you know?

2. What item of clothing do you love the most?

3. What's been your biggest fashion fail?

4. What do you hope will never come back in style?

5. What is your current favourite programme on TV?

6. Who is your favourite band of all time?

7. What's your favourite exercise?

8. What's your favourite song for exercising to?

9. What's your spirit animal?

10.. Which motivates you more, failure or success?

11. What one thing have you been putting off doing?

12. What headline would you like to read in tomorrow's newspaper?

13. What second language would you like to learn?

WHO IN THE WHAT NOW IS ANDY WARHOL?

1. What's your favourite sweets / candy?

2. What's your favourite food?

3. What's your least favourite food?

4. Have you had your fifteen minutes of fame?

5. How do you feel about zoos?

6. What is a perfect day for you?

7. The best dessert in the world?

8. What is your first memory?

9. Who do you look up to most?

10. Have you got rhythm?

11. Can you spell rhythm?

12. Can you whistle?

DON'T TRY TO WALK AND CHEW GUM

1. What's the best piece of advice you've been given?

2. What's a good rule you've learned from your parents?

3. What advice would you give your eight year old self?

5. What do you want for your Birthday?

6. Who would you like to slap with a wet fish?

7. Where do you see yourself in five years?

8. What series did you last binge watch?

9. Which fictional character would you like to hang out with?

10. What fictional place would you like to visit?

11. Name a song that you know the lyrics to.

12. A movie you could watch a hundred times?

13. Your favourite movie as a little kid?

DO THAT CREEPY THING WITH YOUR EARS

1. Do you have any hidden talents?

2. Can you say something in a foreign language?

3. Which country should you live in?

4. What makes you angry?

5. Do you have any special skills?

6. What's your best dance move?

7. What's the biggest surprise you've ever had?

8. What's the best gift you've ever been given?

9. Something people would be surprised to know about you?

10. The most beautiful place you have ever seen?

11. What are you into right now?

12. What do you spend the most money on?

MOM! DON'T CALL ME HONEYBUM IN FRONT OF MY FRIENDS!

1. What's your favourite thing about your parents?

2. What's the coolest fact about your family?

3. Have you ever had a nickname?

4. Do you sing in the shower?

5. Who always made you feel you were a star?

6. Which movie made you cry?

7. When do you feel most beautiful?

8. When do you feel most creative?

9. Favourite song for blasting on family car trips?

10. If you were a song, what would the title be?

11. What type of music are you?

12. Do you believe in angels?

13. What's your musical guilty pleasure?

THE ALGEBRA of CHARISMA
YOUR
INTERESTINGNESS
IS EQUAL TO
YOUR
INTERESTEDNESS.

IF CATS COULD READ, THEY WOULDN'T

1. What's your favourite movie in the last 12 months?

2. If you had a boat what would you call it?

3. What's the last album you listened to?

4. Is there a song your friends would be surprised to know you like?

5. The best word in the English language is...?

6. What's your dream job?

7. What is your most treasured possession?

8. When was the last time you cried?

9. What's your favourite junk food?

10. What's your favourite sport?

11. What's the last song you listened to?

12. Would you rather be fluent in all languages or be able to play every musical instrument?

THIS CITY
IS KILLING ME

1. Your style in one word is…?

2. What is your favourite country?

3. What is your favourite book?

4. What's your favourite place to hang out?

5. What is your guilty pleasure?

6. If you could spend 24 hours with anyone (living or dead) who would it be?

7. You pick up a brass lamp in a thrift store and while cleaning it a genie appears with the "I'll give you three wishes" routine. What do you ask for?

8. Do you believe in ghosts?

9. What language do you wish you could speak?

10. What's the most beautiful thing in the world?

11. What do you collect?

12. Would you rather travel back in time or forward to the future?

13. If you could change one thing in the world right now, what would it be?

I JUST CAN'T HELP BEING QUEEN BEE

1. Which movie would you make a sequel to?

2. What song would be the soundtrack to your life?

3. What would you call your autobiography?

4. Which book do you plan on reading next?

5. What quirky habit do you have?

6. Name one thing on your bucket list.

7. Have you kept any stuffed toys from when you were little?

8. If so, who is your favourite and what did you call it?

8. If you could get on a plane and fly to any country in the world right now, where would you choose to go?

9. Is it worse to be too hot or too cold?

10. Could you live without your phone for a day?

11. Who's your favourite actress?

A WHOLE MESS
OF NACHOS

1. If you absolutely had to enter for an Olympic sport which one would it be?

2. Could you swim a mile?

3. Who taught you to ride a bike?

4. What's the best thing that's happened to you this year?

5. What's your favourite world food?

6. What's your favourite foreign word?

7. What's your least favourite food?

8. Who makes you laugh?

9. Would you ever eat insects?

10. If you could do a cameo in any movie what would it be?

11. What was the last film you saw at the cinema?

12. When was the last time you danced?

13. What is one thing most people don't know about you?

SHOOT FROM THE LIP

This is your chance to open up and through the magic power of spontaneity tell it like it really is.

(The first word that comes into your head)

I am:

I am not:

I love:

I loathe:

I want more:

I want less:

I have:

I have never:

I like:

I don't like:

I'm pretty good at:

I'm rubbish at:

I can:
I can't:

I'm always:
I'm never:

I'm afraid of:
I'm not afraid to:

I need:
I want:

I'm impressed by:
I'm dismayed by:

I'm motivated by:
I'm bored by:

I care about:
I don't care about:

I adore:
I detest:

HELL IS
OTHER PEOPLE

1. Do you like exams?

2. What movie have you watched too many times?

3. You can spend a day of leisure with anyone, who do you choose?

5. Which country do you want to visit next?

6. Who is the most famous person you have met?

7. Who knows you the best?

8. Which superstar would you most like to go on vacation with?

9. If you could go to the refrigerator right now and find one thing, what would you want it to be?

10. How many hats do you own?

11. How many shoes do you own?

12. What's your favourite piece of jewellery?

NO FATE
BUT WHAT WE MAKE

1. Do you believe that your horoscope is accurate?

2. Have you seen a UFO?

3. What makes you cry?

4. What is your favourite food?

5. Favourite thing to eat on the sofa while watching movies?

6. Who was the last person you spoke to?

7. What song makes you get on the dance floor?

8. How many real friends do you have right now?

9. Who is your oldest friend?

10. Who is your oddest friend?

11. What song always makes you happy?

12. Name three apps you use every week.

IT ISN'T REAL
UNTIL IT'S ON TV

1. If you could have a walk on part in any TV series (past or present) what would it be?

2. If you ordered a pizza right now what would it be?

3. Save the money or spend the money?

4. How many places have you lived in?

5. What is your most appealing personality trait?

6. How many true friends are enough?

7. What are you reading?

8. Your best friend just left their diary behind after visiting you, do you read it?

9. If you won 5 million on the lottery, how much would you give to charity?

10. Can you tell me a secret?

11. Can you tell me a lie?

IF A TREE
FALLS IN THE WOODS
AND NOBODY
INSTAGRAMS IT,
DOES IT STILL
MAKE A SOUND?

SHOW
STOPPERS
AND
TOAST
DROPPERS

For those who are sick of small talk
and want to take the conversation deeper.

Drop one of these babies on the table
at the smoothie bar and
watch the conversation blow up.

Use with caution.

May make people think.

HOW DEEP DO YOU DARE TO GO?

Katie looked me in the eye and whispered.
What is love? I dropped my toast...

When you want to ask the kind of question that makes everybody go quiet and look out of the window for a few minutes before they all suddenly erupt at once into an impassioned exchange of ideas and thoughts.

These are the kinds of chats you remember years later. These are the moments your frenemies become friends and your friends become BFF's. These are the times you find yourselves still talking into the small hours of the morning.

You can use these questions as themed sets or you can just grab individual questions that spark your interest. You can ask them as a series or just throw one out to the group when the moment is right.

You have to know when the moment is right.

You have to judge when the people around you are ready to talk. Like, really talk. Y'know?

It's your call.

DOUBLE TAKE.
SAY WHAT?

—

OH NO
YOU BETTER DON'T.

—

OH YOU DID.

THIS is STRICTLY OFF THE RECORD

COMING DIRECTLY
AT YA

Questions considered to be DIRECT
in polite company.

1. Has anyone ever nearly died?

2. What do you spend the most money on?

3. The last time you cried?

4. What is your guilty pleasure?

5. How long does our planet have left?

6. Is a better world possible?

7. How does it feel to fall in love?

8. Is your personality fixed or does it change?

9. Do you have any regrets?

10. Has anyone ever broken a bone?

WORLD PEACE 1

Never ever talk about politics except when are really bored of not having a massive argument with your friends. What are you fighting about!? We're fighting about world peace!!

1. Are you a feminist and what does that mean?

2. Will we ever see world peace in our time?

3. Is it possible to feel love and compassion for people you don't know?

4. Is it possible be a good person?

5. Can you live without hurting other people?

6. Is there enough to go around?

7. Is it wrong to not vote?

8. Can one person make a difference?

9. How do you feel about global warming?

10. How do you define your generation?

11. What are your hopes for the future of your country?

THE DANCE OF THE BROKEN HEART 1

Ain't nothing in the world harder to talk about than love.

1. What is love?

2. Can love last a lifetime?

3. What does it mean to fall in love?

4. Have you ever been in love?

5. Are you in love right now?

6. Is it possible to be in love more than once?

7. Is there a soul mate for everybody?

8. Why is it hard to find love?

9. Can you be in love with someone you've never met?

10. Who are the most in love people you know?

WORLD PEACE 2

Never ever talk about politics except when are really bored of not having a massive argument with your friends. What are you fighting about!? We're fighting about world peace!!

1. What are your hopes for the future of the world?

2. Is it wrong to like having nice things?

3. Can we chase the money and still be good people?

4. Is this world a gift or a test or neither?

5. Do our lives have meaning?

6. Is technology the answer?

7. How would life be different if women ruled the world?

8. Do you think that people should travel? Why?

9. What can you do, starting right now, to make the world a better place?

COMING DIRECTLY
AT YA AGAIN

*Questions considered to be DIRECT
in polite company.*

1. Can bad people ever turn good?

2. What advice would you give to yourself at 10 years old?

3. You are the ruler of the world. What do you do first?

4. Have you ever been bullied?

5. If you were in serious trouble who would you call first?

6. Who in the world understands you the best?

7. How do you want to be seen by others?

8. Is life a game to be won?

THE DANCE OF THE BROKEN HEART 2

*Ain't nothing in the world harder
to talk about than love.*

1. 'Love is a verb. Love is a doing word'. Discuss.

2. What is a broken heart?

3. What's the nicest thing you've ever done for someone else?

4. Would you prefer to be loved by the world or by one human?

5. Can you love someone who lives far away?

6. Do you have a fairytale vision of love?

7. Do you think true love will solve all your problems?

8. What happens after happy ever after?

9. Are there different types of love?

10. Why is there only one word for love in English?

HOW
TO WIN
AT STREAKS

There are over 1000 questions to ask your friends in this book.

If you send them to your friend as snaps, once a day, and they send their answers back as snaps on the same day, you will eventually have the biggest streak in the universe.

Just saying.

1. Take selfie on SC

2. Add text

3. Copy question from book into your snap

4. Send one to best amigos every morning

5. Become Ultimate Streak Master / Mistress!

Please streak responsibly.

SOME QUESTIONS,
YOU ASK THEM A
THOUSAND times
AND THE ANSWER
is ALWAYS THE
SAME:

WHERE ARE YOU FROM?

SOME QUESTIONS
YOU ASK YOU GET
A DIFFERENT
ANSWER EVERY
TIME:

WHERE ARE YOU GOING?